> Erected
> and lighted forever,
> at the expence of
> Edward Simeon Esqr.
> as a mark of affection
> to his native town.
> AD. 1804.
> Lancelot Austwick Esqr.
> Mayor.

So runs the inscription on this prominent vertical feature in Reading's Market Place. It was for many years a forlorn sight, inasmuch as it could be seen at all. Weathered, crumbling and unlit (many younger Readingensians must have been unaware of its original purpose), it was hemmed in by the superstructure of a set of subterranean public lavatories – which were themselves disused for many years before their recent abolition – and prominent road signs. Traffic passed close by on all three sides, and attempts at landscaping in the late 20th century failed to create an enjoyable setting. Ptolemy Dean, visiting in 1996, referred to 'a jostling sea of clutter: reproduction iron bollards, brick paviors of alien colour…'. Now that it has been fully restored and the surroundings visually improved by restricting traffic to the east side of the Market Place, it is perhaps time to review its origin, design, erection, reception and subsequent fate. As we shall see, it caused controversy from the outset and has by no means been universally admired over the last two hundred years.

Naming names

Anyone writing about this structure has first to decide what to call it, juggling the four possible combinations of Soane/Simeon and monument/obelisk. Simeon paid for it, Soane designed it; as Alan Windsor says (see further reading, page 22), strictly it is neither a monument (commemorating nothing and nobody) nor a proper square obelisk in the Egyptian manner, because it is triangular in cross-section. I have favoured Soane, whose greater fame has no doubt saved it from demolition, and obelisk, which is what Simeon asked for.

THE RICH DONOR

Edward Simeon, of a local family, was a director of the Bank of England. No doubt a good banker, he was certainly a real philanthropist: John Man's *History* lists his charities, and he regularly gave clothing to poor children. On the election of a new mayor they were paraded through the Market Place and regaled with a large plum-cake. Simeon was given the Freedom of the Borough in 1805; nevertheless, as we shall see, he was suspected of ulterior motives for his apparent generosity in commissioning the obelisk. On 24 January 1804 he wrote to the Mayor: 'It has very often struck me that the want of light in so great a public spot as the Market Place was productive of inconvenience which every inhabitant and neighbour must experience... request you will make known my desire of erecting at my own expense an obelisk in the centre of the Market Place protected with iron railings and spurs or curb stones to resist the heaviest shock of a waggon. The obelisk to have 4 lamps – to invest in the name of the M[ayor] & B[urgesses] such a sum as will defray for ever the expense of lighting the same during the period when the other public lamps are lighted. The erection will contribute largely to prevent the confusion which now prevails with the wagons on market days by obliging the

Design for Simonds' brewery and brewer's house, 1789.

drivers to take a regular line. The architect will be directed to present the proposed plan…'.

THE MARKET

John Man, Reading's second historian, describes the Market Place in 1816 as 'a spacious open piece of ground, of a triangular form, surrounded by elegant shops for the accommodation of people attending the market, who may be supplied here with colonial or manufactured articles, cheaper than in any other town in the county. This particular spot is kept in repair by the corporation; for which they are entitled to take one pint out of each sack, for all corn sold in the market'. Fruit was sold on Wedesdays, but Saturday was the main event: as well as various grains and legumes you could buy meat, poultry and dairy produce. These latter items had been moved into a new market hall around 1800. Man says that at Michaelmas, the busiest time of year, nearly 200 wagons of produce came to town; some returned empty, others took away stable dung, ashes, chalk and coals.

It is not clear from early views of the Market Place that the obelisk actually improved traffic flow, but the need for artificial light was real. Under the Reading Improvement Act of 1785 (commonly known as the Paving Act) tenders were invited in 1797 for the maintenance of 156 oil-burning public street-lamps; but all of these would have been attached to buildings, leaving pools of darkness in the middle of open spaces such as the Market Place. The OED's first citation for the word 'lamp-post' dates only from 1790, although the Dutch painter Ruisdael had depicted one in a view of Haarlem as early as the 1670s.

THE FAMOUS LOCAL ARCHITECT

The choice of John Soane (later Sir John) as designer is no surprise. He had been appointed architect and surveyor to the Bank of England in 1788, and had some local connexions: born in 1853, probably at Goring or Whitchurch a few miles up the Thames, he was schooled at William Baker's Academy in Reading. In 1789 he built a brewery and house for W B Simonds on Bridge Street – both, alas, totally destroyed in 1900. (Pevsner's 1966 Berkshire volume identifies the present 19 Bridge Street with the brewer's house, but there is plenty of evidence – documents, maps and photographs – to show that this was a different building, closer to the Kennet). In 1794 Soane planned a row of houses for 'London Place', probably where the University's 'red buildings' now stand on London Road; two years later he designed a house for Mayor Austwick next to Greyfriars church, but the finished building – which became the rectory and has since been demolished – differed from his plan, and only some garden walling, gateways and railings may be a relic of Soane. Two other Reading buildings have been locally attributed to him without evidence: 14 St John's Road, known as The Oval,

Design for a house for Lancelot Austwick on Friar Street, 1796

and (more plausibly) Southern Hill at the top of Redlands Road, a gaunt stucco block of six houses pretending to be a villa. This was demolished in 1976.

The design

Most lexicographers insist that obelisks are square, or at least rectangular, in section. The exception is Samuel Johnson, whose definition begins 'a magnificent high piece of solid marble, or other fine stone, having usually four faces…'. Did he know of a triangular specimen in 1755? There are certainly very few post-Reading unsquare examples; probably the most notable is the massive Wellington Monument on the Blackdown Hills, Somerset, designed in 1817 by Thomas Lee. He had spent a brief period in Soane's office in 1810, but a direct influence is unlikely. The triangular base fits the shape of the promontory, but Lee intended it to carry a conventional column; its much-delayed completion took the form of a very plain three-sided obelisk.

Alan Windsor has analysed the probable evolution of the Reading design from drawings in Sir John Soane's Museum. An early idea is conventionally square in plan, with the four lamps that Simeon specified sitting directly on diagonally-set outer piers; the main shaft had Ionic columns at each corner and a cupola on top. The lower half of this version is identical to an unexecuted lamp standard that Soane designed for Norwich Market Place. It would be interesting to know which came first; but the Norwich drawing, is (alas) undated. Soane either re-used the Norwich sketch as a first idea for Reading, or (perhaps less likely) he dug out the rejected early Reading design for Norwich.

The crucial decision to go triangular came very soon. One writer supposed that Soane got this idea from Roman lamps he

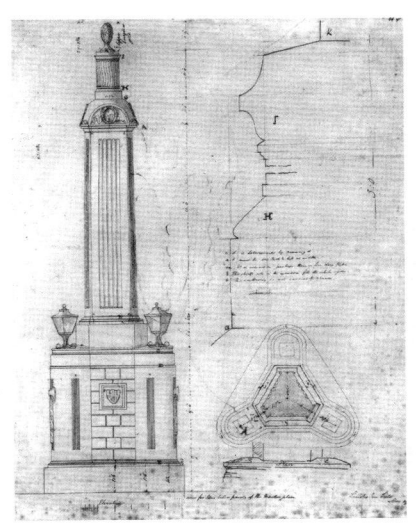

Preliminary designs for the Reading obelisk

had seen at Pompeii; certainly there were what we would now call indoor standard lamps with three feet – as much for stability on uneven floors as for elegance – and in the eighteenth century tall candleholders often took a similar form. But the choice of a three-sided structure in Reading was more likely prompted, as John Man suggests, by the shape of the Market Place itself. Soane had already designed triangular garden structures elsewhere.

When the obelisk was declared a Listed Structure in 1957 the citation described it thus: 'Portland stone fluted obelisk with chamfered sides (key pattern) which have palmette tympana cut into capping. Striated cylinder over capped by pineapple. Rusticated triangular base with lobed corners, each with fasces in relief and with bracketed cast and wrought iron lamp overthrows. Moulded panels on each face – bronze tablet to south inscribed [...]. Contemporary railings, cast iron with fleur de lys heads and heavy standards'. The stone 'pineapple' is actually a less exotic pine-cone – a classical symbol of eternity; Soane intended it to be bronze or gilded copper. The railings have been altered at some stage: the original design was more elaborate, using an 'anthemion' motif of palmetttes alternating with honeysuckle flowers.

BUILDING BEGINS

By 15 May 1804 the Corporation had approved the plan, having no doubt been shown the mahogany model now in the Soane Museum. Soane was in Reading supervising construction on 20 July. Rupert Gunnis's *Dictionary of British Sculptors* tells us that Robert Spiller built the obelisk in 1803 [sic], and was paid £310.3s. According to Dorothy Stroud, James Marshall was the stonemason, J Lovegrove the bricklayer (presumably the stone base clothes a brick core), and Thomas Russell the smith. The lamps and their iron supports were supplied by John Neville, but he was not paid in full; five years later, after his death, his brother threatened to affix a second, shaming plaque to the obelisk:

> 'Edward Simeon Esq. of Salvadore House Accepted from William Neville of Fleet Street £20.9s.7d. as a small donation towards the expense of erecting his obelisk in commemoration of his name for the work and expenses attending the same performed by his late brother John...'.

COMPLETION AND CONTROVERSY

Soane 'surveyed the monument' on 3 September. *The Reading Mercury* did not report its completion or any ceremony; its first mention, on 10 September, is in an account of a venison dinner given by Charles Shaw Lefevre, one of Reading's MPs: 'Mr Monck was remarkably happy in his allusion to a certain newly erected monument, by observing that some gentlemen endeavoured to ingratiate themselves with the Electors by raising monuments of stone, and having their transitory names emblazoned on them in brass...'. The following week a letter from 'An Elector' alleges that '...as to Mr Monck's speech, referring to the Column, it was scarcely touched upon when an almost general hiss marked the wounded feelings of the company, which turned his intended invective into a flowery compliment to Mr Lefevre.' On the 24th 'A Real Elector' replied: '...has not an attempt been made to bias the heads of the Borough in his [Simeon's] favour by setting up in the market-place a paltry gew-gaw thing without use, or name?' He also sarcastically calls the obelisk 'the eighth wonder of the world' and 'a spruce pedestal of Wedgwood Ware, where motley arms and tawdry emblems glare'. Local historians have often quoted the 'gew-gaw' gibe, but not (from delicacy or otherwise) a footnote to the letter, which says 'the writer to whom this is addressed, calls it a column:- perhaps of some new order of architecture, for I never met with a three cornered column among the old ones. Some denominate it an obelisk, others a pillar, but among the generality of the inhabitants, it is called a p****** post.'

The OED defines 'pissing-post' as 'a public urinal, also commonly used for sticking up placards'. As we shall see, the obelisk was not yet lit, and quite likely the railings had not arrived; so that the three shallow recesses – very similar to those of the 'Urilift' pop-up night-time urinal erected round the corner in Town Hall Square in 2002 – would have given a sufficient minimum of privacy for men in need. John Man may well have been the writer, and he certainly had more to say about the obelisk later.

SLEAZE AND BRIBERY

The slurs on Edward Simeon's motives refer to the fact that his brother John, a lawyer and Recorder of Reading 1779-1807, had lost his parliamentary seat in the 1802 election and perhaps needed help to re-establish favour with the electorate. (Only 500 or so of the richest men could vote, so even without corruption the process could hardly have been called democratic.) The *History of Parliament* tells of 'an expensive programme of ostentatious charity and some dubious business transactions'. In the event, John could not fail in the next contest – which was not until 1806 – because in the end only two candidates stood for the two-seat constituency. Nevertheless, according to *Parliament through Seven Centuries* (Aspinall et al, 1962) 'It was said that in 1806 Edward Simeon sent a single ham to voters who split their votes in his [John's] favour, and two hams to those who gave him plumpers [a vote given solely to one candidate]'. John remained MP until 1818 and was made a baronet in 1815. He held reactionary views; he failed to see why the poor should be taught more than one 'R': writing and arithmetic were unnecessary. Reading's own Mary Russell Mitford, who was always good for a pithy thumbnailing, called him 'stationary as Southampton Buildings, solid as the doorpost, and legible as the letters of a brass plate'.

Lighting up

So by late 1804 the obelisk was up, but the lighting arrangements took a little longer to finalize. On 7 January 1805 Edward Simeon wrote to the Mayor:

> 'The building has since been carried out… a variety of experiments has been made in order to produce the most effectual and brilliant light and at length the preference has to be given to burners containing 2 tiers of lights, 3 above and 4 below, each burner containing 36 threads of cotton, so that the 3 lamps are to give a light equal to 27 of the town lamps – as fully explained in the contract with Mr Owen who lights the town lamps – annual charge for lighting and cleaning the lamps £22-5-6. I enclose the bank receipt for £1000 3% – transferred to the mayor and Corporation. Ordered E. Simeon be presented with the freedom of this borough'.

This suggests that the 'gew-gaw' critic, writing three months earlier, may not have realised that lamps were intended, in which case the obelisk could at that date have been fairly called

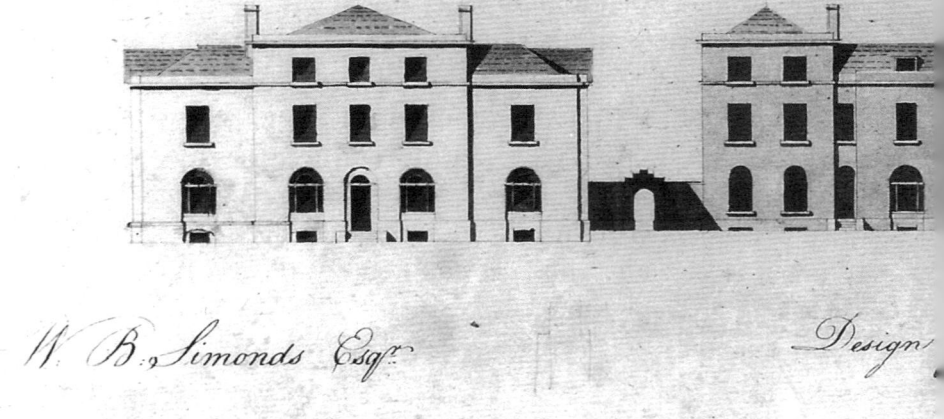

Unexecuted design for houses in London Place, 1794

'without use'. Nearly two years later, the *Mercury* for 24 November 1806 (after John Simeon's election) printed 'An Impromptu on the Obelisk' by 'Readingensis'. Its six stanzas begin:

> Relentless Time shall shake to dust
> This solid monumental stone
> Where, then for fame shall EDWARD trust?
> Oh, to his noble deeds alone.

THE STRANGER'S VIEW

This effort prompted an exchange of squibby anonymous verses in the following four weeks disputing Simeon's generosity. Again, John Man is a suspect on the anti-Simeon side. His anonymously-published *The Stranger in Reading* (1810), a highly critical account of the town supposedly written by a visitor, includes an early example of a Town Trail, in which he notes:

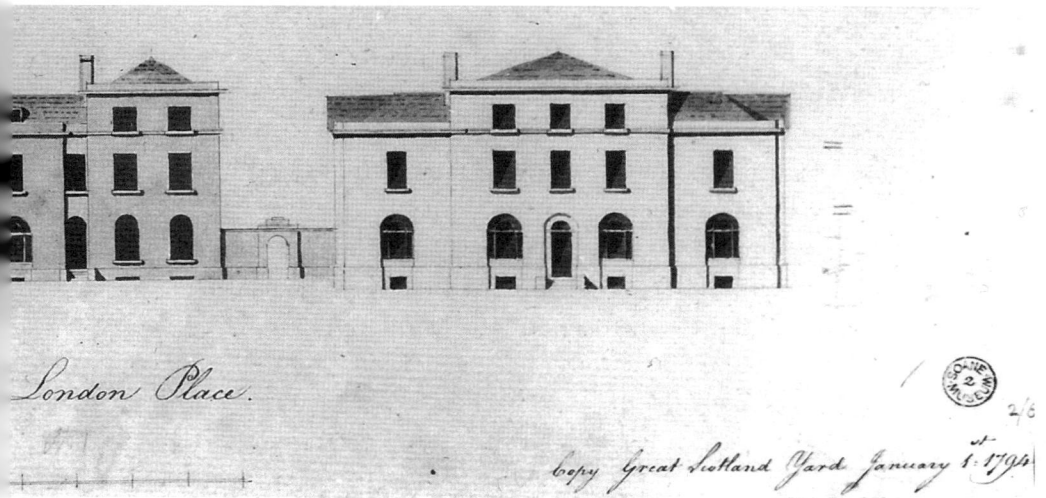

'Nearly in the centre [of the Market Place] is a large stone *lamp post*, if such it may be called, of a triangular form, to correspond, I suppose, with that of the Market-place, but of what order of architecture, I was not able to discover; some of the ornaments however are British, some Roman, and some Egyptian. The base, or pedestal, is, as you may conclude from its shape, divided into three compartments, in one of which, composed of the same kind of gingerbread work I mentioned before, are the town arms, consisting of five maidens' heads placed lozenge wise, the middle one crowned, the others ornamented with garlands of flowers; but I was informed by a great *antiquary*, who resides here, that this was not correct, the original arms having been five maidens' heads, *veiled as nuns*, and not in the meretricious dresses they are here represented; as to the middle one being crowned, he says, it was only introduced in compliment to Queen Elizabeth, who was a great benefactress to the town, and consequently might very well now be omitted. In another compartment are the arms of the founder, and in the third an inscription on a brass plate, recording the time of its erection. The three facets, or corners of the base, are ornamented with what I at first mistook for *bundles of sticks or fagots*, with a woodman's axe thrust into the ends of each of them; but the same learned gentleman assured me, that they were intended to represent the fasces and axes usually carried before the Roman Consuls, in token of their *supreme* power; if so, they are certainly not appropriately introduced here, as the Corporation have only a *delegated*, not a supreme power; they may *whip*, but not *behead* an offender: I would therefore recommend that the axes be taken away, and the fasces left, as being all that is classically necessary to represent that degree of power the Corporation really possess. On the pedestal is raised a triangular shaft, with the facets ornamented in the Egyptian style, and surmounted at the top with something *like an acorn*. At each corner of the pedestal is a large lamp, for the maintenance whereof, for ever, I am told, the founder has funded a sufficient sum of money in annuities, under the management of the Corporation. It is surrounded by a handsome iron railing, and may, upon the whole, be called a pretty, rather than a correct, design for a lamp post.'

Let there be water

Later in the book, in a passage on Reading's water supply, Man makes a facetious proposal:

'Had the worthy gentleman, I mentioned in my former

Watercolour of Market Place published by Shury & Son, c1840

letter, who erected the lamp-post in the Market-place, converted it into a fountain, for the benefit of the neighbourhood, it might have been of incalculable service. To do this, nothing more was wanting, than to have formed the base into a large bason, supplied with cocks at the facets of the three angles, and covered over with a handsome cupola, whereon the shaft might have been erected as it now is, with its accompanying lamp-irons: the whole additional expence would have been in the leaden pipe to convey the water; but, as this would not have required a great bore, perhaps two hundred pounds would have been sufficient to have completed this truly desirable object.'

In the event a pump, protected by two posts, was in due course erected to the south of the obelisk.

Simeon and his money

When Edward Simeon died in 1812, the *Mercury* closed its report of his funeral with an 'Elegy':

> When time has shook the sculptured column's base
> And slander failed true merit to deface
> His praise the teeming mother shall proclame
> Or tender infants, lisping, tell his name.

He left charitable bequests for the benefit of the town totalling £4715, as listed by John Man in his *History*. The £1000 obelisk fund was clearly more than enough to defray the cost of lighting; its administration passed through various bodies over the years, and parts of the capital and income were diverted, at various times, to other good causes: lighting the clock in the Market Place (presumably the one over the 1854 Corn Exchange gateway); The Queen Victoria Institute for Nursing the Sick and Poor of Reading; and the Castle Street Almshouses. The Borough Council took responsibility for the obelisk in 1963, having decided that they could not see the need for an expensive restoration.

Alterations and accretions

Many images of the obelisk have been made over the last 200 years, starting with Robert Dighton's watercolour of 1807. Some are undated, some indulge in artistic licence, and most are general views of the Market Place, so that precise details such as the lamps and railings are hard to make out. But a rough chronology can be constructed, most dates being approximate.

In about 1845 heavier lamp brackets were installed, possibly at the same time as conversion to gas. By 1880 Soane's railings

Market Place and the obelisk decorated for Victoria's Jubilee, 1887

had been replaced by the present ones; from 1890 to 1930 the lamps were mounted on tall posts rising from the ground. A cabman's hut appeared before 1900; its replacement was later used by car park attendants. Lighting was discontinued in 1911 but restored at various dates: in 1971 there were electric mock gas lamps. Before and after that date, the brackets carried baskets of flowers. The underground loos came in 1933: though horribly close to the obelisk, their designer did try to respect its style. A 1941 view shows an air raid shelter – and a long queue of people hoping to secure a rare wartime orange: it was rumoured that 5000 were being delivered. In 1981 the car park was cleared and the obelisk surrounded by curious stone hummocks; the disabled loo was added in 1985.

A Changing Place

The buildings that provide a backdrop to the obelisk have, of course, changed a great deal over the last 200 years. The only survivors from 1804 are the mediaeval St Laurence, nos. 27-28 and the Coopers (all 17th century, though the latter has clearly been refronted) and nos. 48-49 (18th century). No.52 is roughly contemporary with the obelisk; all else is later. Much was lost to the grim 1960s arcades, which were intended to march all the way round.

The selection of shops and trades, too, has varied considerably. In 1906 you could still enjoy a fairly complete retail experience: there were a chemist, a shoemaker, a cycle depot and (very up-to-date) a motor agent, a wine and spirit merchant, retailers of tea, coffee, rubberware, china and glassware, two tobacconists, three tailors, a fishmonger/poulterer/game dealer, two booksellers (one also a printer), a seed merchant (Suttons, of course, whose gothic frontage led into their vast establishment between the Forbury and the King's Road), a draper/mercer/hosier who doubled as an undertaker, a hairdresser with a sideline in fishing tackle, a solicitor, an accountant and four architects, banks, estate agents, insurers, a Pickfords (carriers, removers and tourist agents), the Elephant Hotel and the Feathers, the offices of the Reading Mercury, and the headquarters of the local Conservative Association.

A century on, the offer is very limited: the banks are still there, joined by a Post Office; there's a pub (which doesn't do accommodation); you can have a haircut and a tan, buy bread, sandwiches, hi-fi, a guitar, or second-hand clothes and bric-a-brac from the charity shop; you can have your dry cleaning done and rent an office in Soane Point. The market itself went to Hosier Street in 1973, the same year that Suttons finally closed their shop.

Market Place, 1968

OPINIONS AND CAMPAIGNS

John Man was not alone in his less than favourable opinion of the obelisk, though in a chapter on local worthies in *The Stranger*, he admitted that Soane was 'one of [London's] first architects' and admired his 'superior abilities'. J J Cooper's *Worthies of Reading* (1923) says 'One is bound to admit that opinions regarding its beauty vary considerably, but those who do not greatly admire this conspicuous feature of our Market Place willingly concede that as a lamp pedestal it has for many a long night seemed a cheerful enlightenment to belated wayfarers.' Alan Wykes, in *Reading, a Biography* (1970) calls it 'a thing of no great beauty.' In 1996 Peter Hay, artist and founder of Two Rivers Press, was thinking of publishing 'a speculative illustrated pamphlet' about this 'justifiably ignored and unpopular decaying Portland stone "obelisk".' And Keith Miller, writing in the *Daily Telegraph* in 2003, describes 'a strange, tripodal stalk of limestone ... all that is left is a rather clumsy bit of masonry, revered by Soane fans, ignored by everyone else. Maybe they should dig it up and move it to the forecourt of the Hexagon theatre, where its obscure iconography could find a new significance among snooker fans'.

But the obelisk did have its admirers, and there were others who did not consider it a masterpiece but agreed that it must be preserved as an example of the work of a hugely important architect. In 1966 the fledgling Reading Civic Society pleaded for lighting to be restored; a decade later Robert Horsnell campaigned for improvements to its setting (at that time a vast road-sign obscured the north aspect); and the Soane Monuments Trust sought a full restoration. In 2005 the Council approved a scheme for new landscaping and street furniture, to be followed by restoration of the obelisk in accordance with plans drawn up by Julian Harrap Architects.

Soane's legacy and reputation

John Soane did achieve fame in his own time, and was recognised as the leading architect of his latter days; but he was unfortunate in many of his clients, who meddled with his designs, passed them on to lesser men to carry out, or cancelled their commissions altogether. (Though some of his problems may have stemmed from his own character: John Summerson calls him 'a curious, thorny, intricate personality'.) The list of his projects in Dorothy Stroud's book is a very sad read: apart from the many unexecuted designs, the words 'demolished' and 'remodelled' are appended to a substantial proportion of what he did build. In other cases only minor alterations or outbuildings survive. He died in 1837, just after A W N Pugin had published his *Contrasts*, in which he reviled all neo-classicists, pointedly including some of Soane's works in his rogues' gallery; in 1843 his *Apology for the Revival of Christian Architecture in England* declares that 'We are just emerging from a state which may be

–20–

Market Place, c1970

termed the dark ages of architecture.' The Gothic Revival was soon sweeping across the land. There was no Soane 'school'; his smaller houses were often very plain outside, and not considered worth saving. Even the Bank, his spectacular masterpiece, was almost totally destroyed by Herbert Baker between 1923 and 1939. As late as 1954, Banister Fletcher's *History of Architecture* still approved this vandalism and criticised Soane, as had the first edition of this standard reference book 58 years earlier: 'His designs are those of an original mind, but he was unable to clothe them with suitable details. There is a consequent taint of eccentricity'. (Nicholas Hawksmoor, another genius working a century earlier, was similarly condemned: 'Ideas, of some originality and grandeur, are too often marred by eccentricities of treatment'.)

REHABILITATION AND INFLUENCE

But tastes change, and in 1957 Pevsner described the Bank job as 'the worst individual loss suffered by London's architecture in the 20th century'. (And this was in peacetime!) Soane's genius is now fully appreciated, and many modern architects acknowledge the influence of his style and his mastery of space. New art galleries reinterpret his pioneering one at Dulwich; and his trademark pendentive or handkerchief dome, found in the tiny breakfast room at 13 Lincoln's Inn Fields, crops up in St John's College, Oxford, a cultural centre in Murcia, Spain, a synagogue in New York, a hall in Tokyo, and even in the Bluewater shopping centre in Kent. But the most familiar example in Britain is Giles Gilbert Scott's classic 1924 red public telephone kiosk; only a small fraction of the 60,000 made have survived (and most are listed). The design is both pleasing and practical: it directs rainwater to the corners. It happens that two examples of the current melted-plastic version of the kiosk sit in the Market Place a few yards from the obelisk – which itself carries a triangular version of the dome at the top of its main shaft.

The places where one can have a reasonably complete 'Soane Experience' are few: his Museum in Lincoln's Inn Fields; Pitzhanger Manor, Ealing (his country home); the Dulwich Art Gallery; and his family tomb in Old St Pancras churchyard. The obelisk is just about all that is left of him in Reading, and it is entirely right that it is now fully restored in a sympathetic setting, and that Edward Simeon's wishes – whatever his motives in 1804 – are once again respected. May it now indeed be maintained and lighted forever.

FURTHER READING

I am greatly indebted to Alan Windsor, who wrote a very full account of the obelisk – 'The Simeon monument in Reading by Sir John Soane' – in *English Architecture Public and Private*, edited by Bold and Chaney (1993). The standard general work

Obelisk, toilet vent and Corn Exchange entrance, 1996

on Soane is Dorothy Stroud's *Sir John Soane, Architect* (second edition, 1996). The Soane Museum has staged many exhibitions over the years, accompanied by scholarly catalogues. That for 'Soane Revisited' (1996) contains drawings made in Reading by Ptolemy Dean during a journey in search of the master's lesser-known works; 'Inspired by Soane' (1999) describes numerous 20th century buildings by distinguished architects who acknowledge his influence. For accounts of Reading around the time of the obelisk's erection, the three primary sources are the *Histories* by Coates (1802) and Man (1816), and the latter's *The Stranger in Reading* (1810), available in a new illustrated edition from Two Rivers Press (2005).

Acknowledgements:
Soane's drawings are reproduced by courtesy of the Trustees of Sir John Soane's Museum; the photos of Market Place in the 20th century appear by permission of the Reading Evening Post.

For assistance of various kinds I have to thank David Cliffe and Reading Libraries, Matthew Williams and the Museum of Reading, the Berkshire Record Office, Sidney Gold, Alison Bennett and Adam Stout.

Book design & cover illustrations © Sally Castle 2007
www.sallycastle.co.uk

Printed by
Genesis Impressions Ltd, Reading, Berkshire

First published in the UK by
Two Rivers Press 35–39 London Street Reading RG1 4PS
www.tworiverspress.com
Two Rivers Press is a member of Inpress

Copyright © Adam Sowan 2007
The right of Adam Sowan to be identified as the author of this work has been asserted by him in accordance with the Copyright, Designs and Patents Act of 1988

ISBN 978-1-901677-51-5

Other books by Adam Sowan & published by Two Rivers Press:
A Much-Maligned Town: Opinions of Reading 1586–1997;
Abattoirs Road to Zinzan Street: Reading's Streets and their Names; The Holy Brook, or the Granator's Tale.